MARSHALL MEYER

ChatGPT for Entrepreneurs

Revolutionize Your Business Strategy with AI-Powered Insights and Innovation (2024 Beginner's Guide)

Copyright © 2024 by Marshall Meyer

All rights reserved. No part of this publication may be reproduced, stored or transmitted in any form or by any means, electronic, mechanical, photocopying, recording, scanning, or otherwise without written permission from the publisher. It is illegal to copy this book, post it to a website, or distribute it by any other means without permission.

First edition

This book was professionally typeset on Reedsy.
Find out more at reedsy.com

Contents

1. Introduction to ChatGPT for Entrepreneurs — 1
2. Market Research with ChatGPT — 6
3. Idea Generation and Validation — 10
4. Business Planning and Strategy — 15
5. Using ChatGPT for Marketing and Advertising — 20
6. Customer Service Automation — 25
7. ChatGPT for Product Development — 30
8. Improving Operational Efficiency — 34
9. ChatGPT for HR and Team Management — 38
10. Looking Ahead: ChatGPT and the Future of Entrepreneurship — 43

1

Introduction to ChatGPT for Entrepreneurs

ChatGPT, created by OpenAI, is a robust language model built upon the GPT framework, with the aim of comprehending and producing text akin to human language. Entrepreneurs can utilize ChatGPT to improve different facets of their businesses, including idea generation, content creation, customer support, and more. Here's an overview of how entrepreneurs can leverage ChatGPT:

1. Idea generation and brainstorming: ChatGPT serves as a valuable tool for generating fresh ideas and brainstorming solutions for business challenges. By initiating prompts or posing questions, entrepreneurs can employ ChatGPT to explore novel business concepts, product ideas, marketing strategies, or operational enhancements.
2. Content creation: ChatGPT aids in crafting diverse content types like blog posts, social media updates, marketing copy, product descriptions, or email templates. By providing initial input or guidelines, entrepreneurs can produce high-quality content tailored to their business requirements with minimal effort.
3. Market research and analysis: Entrepreneurs can utilize ChatGPT to assist in analyzing market trends, industry reports, or customer feedback.

By posing specific questions, entrepreneurs can gain insights into their target audience, competitors, and potential opportunities or challenges in their market.

4. Customer support: ChatGPT can be integrated into chatbots or customer support systems, enabling entrepreneurs to offer efficient and personalized assistance to their customers. This can lead to improved customer satisfaction, reduced response times, and more time for support teams to tackle complex issues.
5. Task automation: ChatGPT can automate various tasks like generating meeting summaries, organizing to-do lists, or managing email correspondence. By automating routine tasks, entrepreneurs can save time and concentrate on more strategic aspects of their business.
6. Personalized experiences: ChatGPT aids entrepreneurs in creating personalized experiences for their customers, such as customized product recommendations or targeted marketing campaigns. By understanding user preferences and needs, ChatGPT can generate content that resonates with the target audience, ultimately driving engagement and conversions.

To maximize the potential of ChatGPT, entrepreneurs should familiarize themselves with the OpenAI API, which grants access to the model and facilitates integration with various applications. By exploring the potential use cases and benefits of ChatGPT, entrepreneurs can harness the power of AI to enhance their business operations, foster innovation, and gain a competitive edge.

Understanding ChatGPT

ChatGPT, developed by OpenAI, is an advanced language model based on the GPT (Generative Pre-trained Transformer) architecture. It's engineered to comprehend and produce human-like text, serving as a versatile tool across many domains. To grasp ChatGPT, let's delve into its fundamental elements and functionalities:

1. GPT Architecture: GPT, short for Generative Pre-trained Transformer, is an AI model utilizing the Transformer architecture. This design is tailored for processing sequential data, such as text, and involves pre-training the model on extensive text datasets before fine-tuning it for specific tasks.
2. Generative Model: ChatGPT operates as a generative model, capable of generating text based on provided input. It achieves this by predicting subsequent words in a sequence, considering the given context. This ability lends itself well to tasks like content generation, summarization, and translation.
3. Contextual Understanding: Designed with a focus on contextual comprehension, ChatGPT can grasp the relationships between words, phrases, and sentences. This enables it to produce coherent and contextually relevant responses, establishing its prowess as a conversational AI.
4. Fine-tuning: Despite being pre-trained on extensive data, ChatGPT can undergo fine-tuning for specific domains or tasks. This adaptability allows it to excel in various applications, from customer support to content creation and natural language processing.
5. Prompt-based Interaction: ChatGPT operates through prompts, which are textual inputs provided by users. These prompts guide the model's responses, which are generated based on both the provided context and the model's language understanding.
6. Token-based Processing: ChatGPT processes text in tokens, which can range from single characters to words depending on the language. The model's token-handling capability determines its efficiency in processing longer or more complex texts.

By comprehending these core aspects of ChatGPT, one can appreciate its diverse applications and capabilities. ChatGPT has showcased remarkable performance across various natural language processing tasks, making it an invaluable asset for businesses, researchers, and developers alike.

Importance of AI in Entrepreneurship

Utilizing AI has become increasingly crucial for entrepreneurs, offering a plethora of advantages and avenues for business advancement, innovation, and competitiveness within the market. The significance of AI for entrepreneurs can be summarized as follows:

1. Enhanced Decision-making: AI possesses the capability to swiftly and accurately analyze extensive datasets, furnishing invaluable insights that facilitate informed decision-making. By harnessing AI-driven analytics, entrepreneurs can make data-informed decisions that enhance business performance and mitigate potential risks.
2. Enhanced Efficiency: AI has the potential to automate repetitive tasks and streamline operational workflows, thereby liberating time for entrepreneurs and their teams to concentrate on strategic endeavors. This heightened efficiency can result in cost reductions and heightened productivity.
3. Personalization and Customer Engagement: AI empowers businesses to deliver personalized experiences to their clientele, customizing marketing campaigns, product recommendations, and customer service interactions based on individual preferences and needs. This fosters customer loyalty, elevates engagement, and drives sales.
4. Innovation and Product Development: AI aids in the generation of novel concepts, identification of market prospects, and acceleration of product development cycles. Entrepreneurs can leverage AI technologies to craft innovative products and services that cater to customer demands and distinguish their enterprises in the market.

5. Competitive Edge: Early adoption of AI confers a competitive edge by enabling businesses to remain abreast of industry trends, react promptly to market shifts, and furnish superior customer experiences.
6. Enhanced Customer Support: AI-powered chatbots and support systems offer swift, precise, and personalized assistance to customers, heightening satisfaction levels, reducing support expenses, and boosting customer retention rates.
7. Scalability: AI facilitates more efficient business scalability by automating processes, analyzing data, and optimizing operations, thereby enabling entrepreneurs to expand their enterprises more effectively, even with constrained resources.
8. Risk Management: AI aids entrepreneurs in identifying and mitigating potential risks by monitoring real-time data, identifying anomalies, and forecasting trends. This is particularly invaluable in domains like cybersecurity, fraud detection, and supply chain management.
9. Talent Management: AI supports human resource functions by streamlining recruitment processes, identifying skill gaps, and furnishing personalized training and development opportunities for employees.

To fully capitalize on the potential of AI in entrepreneurship, it is imperative for business proprietors to stay abreast of the latest AI advancements, invest in AI-powered tools and solutions, and devise an AI strategy aligned with their business objectives. By embracing AI, entrepreneurs can unlock novel growth opportunities, foster innovation, and achieve success.

2

Market Research with ChatGPT

Utilizing ChatGPT for market research can be immensely beneficial for entrepreneurs seeking to understand their target audience, competitors, and industry trends. Here's how you can employ ChatGPT effectively in market research:

1. Customer feedback analysis: Utilize ChatGPT to process and interpret customer feedback from various sources like reviews, social media comments, or surveys. By prompting the model to summarize key points or detect common themes, valuable insights into customer preferences, pain points, and improvement areas can be gained.
2. Competitor assessment: ChatGPT can aid in evaluating competitors by generating summaries of their product offerings, marketing strategies, strengths, and weaknesses. Furnish the model with competitor data and ask it to compare them to your business or uncover potential differentiation opportunities.
3. Trend monitoring: Stay abreast of industry trends and emerging technologies using ChatGPT to process and summarize relevant articles, reports, or news stories. Task the model with identifying significant trends and insights to ensure your business remains adaptable to market shifts.

4. Target audience identification: Employ ChatGPT to define your target audience by analyzing demographic data, customer profiles, or user personas. Task the model with identifying common characteristics, needs, or preferences among your target customers to tailor your products and marketing efforts accordingly.
5. Market research question generation: Develop a comprehensive market research plan with ChatGPT's assistance by generating pertinent questions for surveys, interviews, or focus groups. Provide the model with your research objectives to receive a list of questions aimed at gathering necessary insights for your business.
6. Findings summarization: Post conducting market research, utilize ChatGPT to summarize findings concisely and clearly. This aids in effectively communicating insights to stakeholders or team members and informs strategic decision-making.

While ChatGPT serves as a valuable market research tool, it's essential to acknowledge its limitations in providing accurate or up-to-date information due to its training data being limited to data up until September 2021. Cross-referencing and verifying information generated by ChatGPT with other sources are crucial to ensure the validity and reliability of market research findings.

Utilizing ChatGPT to Discern Trends

Utilizing ChatGPT can be advantageous for recognizing trends across diverse sectors, markets, or subjects. To effectively utilize ChatGPT for trend spotting, adhere to these steps:

1. Clearly define your aim: Articulate the objective of your trend analysis, such as pinpointing emerging technologies within a specific sector or grasping consumer inclinations in a particular market.

2. Gather data: Compile pertinent data sources like articles, reports, news items, or social media content relevant to your subject. Utilize this data as input for ChatGPT to ensure it possesses adequate context for generating meaningful insights.
3. Craft prompts: Devise prompts that steer ChatGPT towards furnishing the desired information. For instance, prompt the model to "recognize key trends in the [industry] over the last two years" or "summarize notable shifts in consumer preferences for [product category]." Ensure your prompts are precise and unambiguous.
4. Evaluate responses: Examine the responses generated by ChatGPT and identify recurring themes, patterns, or insights conducive to trend identification. Be ready to refine your prompts or provide additional context if initial responses are unsatisfactory.
5. Cross-check and authenticate: Given ChatGPT's knowledge limitation to training data up until September 2021, it's imperative to corroborate the identified trends with other sources for accuracy and relevance. Consult recent reports, articles, or expert opinions to validate the trends highlighted by ChatGPT.
6. Condense and convey findings: Once you've discerned and verified the trends, utilize ChatGPT to summarize your findings. This facilitates effective communication of insights to stakeholders, team members, or clients.

By adhering to these steps and harnessing ChatGPT's robust natural language processing capabilities, you can identify trends that inform your business decisions, marketing strategies, or product development endeavors. Remember, ChatGPT should supplement other research methods, and its outputs should always be corroborated and complemented by other sources to ensure a comprehensive understanding of trends in your field of interest.

Examining Market Information

Examining market data plays a crucial role in making well-informed business decisions. Although ChatGPT excels in textual analysis, it isn't tailored for processing numerical market data. Nevertheless, it can still aid in comprehending the data's implications or deriving insights from provided information.

Here's how you can utilize ChatGPT for market data analysis:

1. Condensing findings: Post analyzing market data with specialized tools, you can furnish ChatGPT with a brief overview of your discoveries and request a succinct summary or highlighting key points.
2. Generating insights: Share your market data analysis outcomes with ChatGPT and solicit insights or recommendations based on the data. For instance, inquire about potential marketing strategies aligned with current market trends and customer preferences.
3. Interpreting data: Employ ChatGPT to help decipher specific data points or metrics. For example, seek clarification on the implications of a high churn rate for your business and ways to enhance customer retention.
4. Detecting patterns or irregularities: Although ChatGPT isn't geared for direct numerical data processing, you can describe observed patterns or anomalies in the data and seek explanations or suggestions for addressing them.
5. Forecasting: While ChatGPT isn't explicitly designed for forecasting, you can supply it with historical market data and request potential future trends or scenarios. However, it's vital to validate and cross-reference these predictions with other forecasting methods or expert opinions.

Remember, ChatGPT's forte lies in natural language processing rather than numerical analysis. To effectively analyze market data, leverage specialized tools like Excel, Tableau, or Power BI, and consult industry experts or reports to ensure the accuracy and reliability of your findings.

3

Idea Generation and Validation

Developing new products, services, or strategies requires crucial steps in idea generation and validation. Utilizing ChatGPT proves beneficial in both phases. Here's how to leverage ChatGPT for these purposes:

For Idea Generation:

1. Employ brainstorming prompts: Kickstart by furnishing ChatGPT with a prompt outlining your goals, like "Generate innovative product ideas for the sustainable fashion industry." Precision in prompts aids the model in producing pertinent ideas.
2. Explore varied perspectives: Foster diverse ideas by prompting ChatGPT to consider different viewpoints or user personas. For instance, inquire, "What product feature would busy professionals find valuable in the sustainable fashion industry?"
3. Overcome creative hurdles: Combat specific challenges or aspects of your idea by seeking suggestions or alternative approaches from ChatGPT. This aids in surmounting creative blocks and uncovering novel solutions.
4. Iterate and enhance: Continuously refine prompts to elicit more detailed or targeted ideas. Additionally, offer feedback on generated ideas to

steer the model towards improved suggestions.

For Idea Validation:

1. Evaluate feasibility: After compiling a list of ideas, utilize ChatGPT to assess their feasibility by querying, "What challenges might arise in implementing this idea?" or "What resources are necessary to materialize this idea?"
2. Analyze market suitability: Assess the idea's alignment with current sustainable fashion industry trends or its target audience's preferences and needs using ChatGPT.
3. Assess competition: Employ ChatGPT to analyze competitors by requesting identification and assessment of their strengths and weaknesses concerning the proposed product.
4. Estimate impact: Task ChatGPT with estimating the potential impact of your idea considering customer benefits, revenue projections, and environmental implications.
5. Gather feedback: Generate questions for surveys, interviews, or focus groups using ChatGPT to collect input from potential users, stakeholders, or industry experts.

Although ChatGPT serves as a valuable aid in idea generation and validation, it's crucial to acknowledge its knowledge limitations, extending only until September 2021. Always corroborate ChatGPT-generated information with other sources and seek expert advice or conduct additional research to ensure the accuracy and relevance of findings.

Brainstorming Business Ideas with ChatGPT

Utilizing ChatGPT for brainstorming business concepts can be advantageous, offering a stream of imaginative suggestions and perspectives. To effectively engage in this process, adhere to these steps:

1. Clarify your objective: Clearly state the purpose of your brainstorming, whether it's pinpointing opportunities within an industry or crafting a novel product/service concept.
2. Craft prompts: Develop prompts that guide ChatGPT towards furnishing pertinent and beneficial ideas. For instance, request the model to propose "innovative business ventures for the healthcare sector" or "methods to combat plastic waste sustainably." Ensure your prompts are specific and unambiguous.
3. Explore various perspectives: Encourage ChatGPT to delve into different angles by considering diverse user personas, market segments, or viewpoints. Pose questions such as "What business concepts address the needs of remote workers?" or "What sustainable opportunities exist in the food and beverage realm?"
4. Iterate and refine: Be open to refining your prompts or providing additional context if the initial responses are inadequate. Offering feedback on generated ideas can steer the model towards better suggestions.
5. Assess and narrow down ideas: Evaluate ChatGPT's generated ideas and pinpoint those with the most promise. Factors such as market demand, feasibility, competition, and alignment with your resources, skills, and goals should be considered.
6. Conduct further research and validation: Once promising ideas are identified, conduct thorough research and seek validation from industry reports, experts, or potential customers to refine and validate them.

Remember, ChatGPT serves as a supplementary tool for brainstorming, and its outputs should be supplemented with other research methods to ensure a comprehensive understanding of business opportunities and challenges. Leveraging ChatGPT's robust natural language processing capabilities can ignite creative business ideas and uncover new market opportunities, thus enriching your entrepreneurial journey.

IDEA GENERATION AND VALIDATION

Utilizing ChatGPT for Idea Validation

Although ChatGPT can serve as a valuable asset for validating ideas, it's important to acknowledge its limitations, as it relies on training data only up to September 2021. Nevertheless, ChatGPT can aid in assessing ideas from various angles and prompting relevant inquiries. Here's how you can leverage ChatGPT for idea validation:

1. Evaluate Feasibility: Pose questions to ChatGPT concerning the feasibility of your concept. For instance, inquire about potential hurdles in launching a subscription-based meal kit service or the resources needed for developing a virtual reality fitness app.
2. Assess Market Fit: Utilize ChatGPT to comprehend the alignment of your idea with market trends. You might ask about current online education trends and how a gamified learning platform fits into them or about the target demographic and preferences for an eco-friendly cleaning product.
3. Analyze Competition: Interrogate ChatGPT about competitors in your space, their strengths, weaknesses, and how to differentiate your offering from existing solutions.
4. Identify Risks: Seek ChatGPT's input on potential risks like regulatory challenges, market saturation, or technological barriers.
5. Estimate Impact: Request ChatGPT's assistance in estimating the impact of your idea, considering factors such as customer benefits, revenue potential, and societal or environmental implications.
6. Gather Feedback: Generate questions using ChatGPT for surveys, interviews, or focus groups to solicit feedback from stakeholders, potential users, or industry experts.
7. Refine Idea: Utilize insights and feedback from ChatGPT to refine your idea, identifying areas for enhancement, optimizing features, or addressing challenges.

While ChatGPT serves as a valuable tool, it shouldn't be your sole validation source. It's crucial to corroborate ChatGPT-generated insights with other sources such as industry reports, expert opinions, and customer feedback. By combining ChatGPT's capabilities with other research methods, you can enhance the effectiveness of idea validation and make well-informed decisions regarding your business, product, or service.

4

Business Planning and Strategy

Utilizing ChatGPT can be advantageous for aiding various aspects of business planning and strategy. Here's how you can harness ChatGPT for this purpose:

1. Market examination: Utilize ChatGPT to scrutinize market patterns, customer inclinations, and competitors. Pose inquiries like, "What are the current trends in the renewable energy market?" or "Who are the primary competitors for an online coaching platform?"
2. Identifying target demographic: ChatGPT can assist in defining your target audience based on your product or service. For instance, inquire, "What are the characteristics of the target audience for a luxury skincare brand?"
3. SWOT analysis: ChatGPT can facilitate a SWOT analysis of your business. Furnish the model with your business details and request it to highlight the key aspects of your SWOT analysis.
4. Establishing objectives: Utilize ChatGPT to formulate SMART objectives for your business. For instance, ask, "What are some SMART objectives for a new e-commerce store selling eco-friendly products?"
5. Brainstorming strategies: Utilize ChatGPT to generate potential strategies for achieving your business objectives. For example, inquire, "What are some marketing strategies to boost the online visibility of our mobile

app?" or "What are some cost-effective methods to enhance customer retention?"
6. Risk assessment: ChatGPT can aid in identifying potential risks or challenges associated with your business plan. Pose questions like, "What are some potential risks in expanding our business internationally?" or "What are the potential challenges of implementing a remote work model for our company?"
7. Crafting action plans: Seek assistance from ChatGPT in developing action plans to execute your strategies or achieve your objectives. For instance, ask, "What are the steps to execute a successful crowdfunding campaign?" or "How can we optimize our supply chain to cut costs and enhance efficiency?"
8. Financial planning: Although ChatGPT isn't specifically designed for financial analysis, you can still utilize it to generate inquiries or considerations for your financial planning. For example, ask, "What are the key financial metrics to monitor for our SaaS business?" or "What are some strategies to enhance cash flow management?"

Remember, ChatGPT's knowledge is confined to its training data up to September 2021. Always cross-reference the information from ChatGPT with other sources and seek expert advice or conduct additional research to ensure the accuracy and relevance of your findings. By leveraging ChatGPT's capabilities alongside other research methods, you can devise more informed and effective business plans and strategies.

Creating Strategic Business Blueprints Alongside ChatGPT

Utilizing ChatGPT can be a valuable aid in crafting business plans by offering insights, advice, and cues to streamline the process. Here's a step-by-step guide on harnessing ChatGPT for business plan development:

1. Define your business: Provide ChatGPT with a concise overview of your business, its goals, and the audience it aims to serve.
2. Market analysis: Employ ChatGPT to gain understanding into market dynamics, consumer preferences, and competition within your sector. Pose queries like, "What current trends influence the e-commerce landscape?" or "Who are the primary competitors in the healthy food delivery niche?"
3. Unique value proposition: Solicit ChatGPT's assistance in pinpointing and articulating your business's unique value proposition that distinguishes it from rivals. For instance, inquire, "What sets apart a sustainable fashion brand?"
4. SWOT analysis: Utilize ChatGPT to construct a SWOT analysis (Strengths, Weaknesses, Opportunities, and Threats) for your venture. Offer pertinent details about your business and prompt it to identify key elements of the analysis.
5. Crafting a marketing strategy: Seek ChatGPT's guidance in formulating a marketing strategy aligned with your business objectives and target demographic. For example, ask, "Which marketing channels are optimal for reaching the luxury travel market?"
6. Financial projections: Although not tailored for financial analysis, leverage ChatGPT to generate queries or considerations for your financial forecasts, such as revenue streams for a software-as-a-service (SaaS) enterprise or typical expenses for a small retail operation.
7. Operational processes: Enlist ChatGPT's help in delineating critical operational processes, including supply chain management, logistics,

and customer service, crucial for your business's prosperity.
8. Setting milestones: Utilize ChatGPT to establish SMART (Specific, Measurable, Achievable, Relevant, and Time-bound) objectives and milestones for your business plan.
9. Iteration and refinement: Review and refine your business plan with ChatGPT's insights and feedback. Continuously iterate on prompts or request additional questions to enhance your plan's efficacy.

While ChatGPT serves as a valuable tool, it's imperative not to rely solely on it for business plan development. Cross-referencing ChatGPT's insights with other sources such as industry reports, expert opinions, and customer feedback ensures the accuracy and relevance of your findings. By combining ChatGPT's capabilities with other research methods, you can craft comprehensive and effective business plans aligned with your objectives and target audience.

Effective Planning and Prediction

Efficient planning and prediction play pivotal roles in the success of any business venture. Utilizing ChatGPT can significantly aid in these endeavors by offering valuable insights, data analysis, and forecasts. Here's a breakdown of how ChatGPT can be employed for strategic planning and forecasting:

1. **Understanding Market Trends:** ChatGPT can help decipher current and future market trends within your industry. Pose queries like "What emerging technologies are prevalent in the renewable energy sector?" or "What market opportunities are foreseeable in the e-learning industry?"

2. **Forecasting Demand:** By factoring in variables such as market size, consumer behavior, and competition, ChatGPT can assist in predicting the demand for your product or service. Questions like "What demand can we

expect for our product over the next three years?" or "How might consumer behavior shift in response to the pandemic?" can be explored.

3. **Risk Identification:** Engage ChatGPT to identify and evaluate potential risks or obstacles that could affect your business in the future. For instance, inquire about the risks associated with expanding internationally or potential regulatory changes impacting your industry.

4. **Scenario Development:** ChatGPT aids in devising various business scenarios based on different assumptions and variables. For example, assess the potential revenue impact of increasing advertising spending by 50% or explore best-case and worst-case sales scenarios for the upcoming year.

5. **Opportunity Evaluation:** Evaluate potential business opportunities by considering factors such as market demand, competition, and available resources. Questions like "What benefits might we gain from entering a new market segment?" or "How can we diversify our revenue streams?" can be explored.

6. **Financial Projections:** Generate financial projections with ChatGPT based on specified assumptions and data inputs. Query about projected revenue and expenses over the next few years or the return on investment for a new product launch.

7. **Strategy Development:** Utilize insights provided by ChatGPT to formulate strategies and action plans aligned with your objectives and responsive to potential risks or opportunities.

Remember to corroborate ChatGPT's insights with other sources and expert opinions due to its training data being limited up to September 2021. By integrating ChatGPT's capabilities with other research methodologies, you can develop more informed and efficacious strategic plans and forecasts tailored to your business objectives and target audience.

5

Using ChatGPT for Marketing and Advertising

Utilizing ChatGPT can greatly aid in multiple facets of marketing and advertising endeavors, offering valuable insights, recommendations, and content concepts. Here's a breakdown of how you can utilize ChatGPT for marketing and advertising purposes:

1. Defining Target Audience: Utilize ChatGPT to assist in defining and comprehending your target audience based on factors like demographics, behavior, and preferences. For instance, inquire about the characteristics or preferences of the target audience for specific products or services.
2. Crafting Brand Messaging: Engage ChatGPT to develop clear and captivating brand messaging tailored to resonate with your target audience. This could involve seeking input on key value propositions or effective taglines.
3. Generating Content Ideas: Leverage ChatGPT to brainstorm and generate diverse content ideas suitable for various marketing and advertising campaigns, encompassing blog posts, social media content, or video ads.
4. Analyzing Customer Feedback: Seek ChatGPT's assistance in analyzing customer feedback such as reviews or social media comments to identify

areas for improvement or opportunities to enhance marketing efforts.
5. Optimizing Advertising Campaigns: Utilize ChatGPT to optimize advertising campaigns by generating suggestions for targeting, ad copy, or design elements, ensuring they effectively reach and engage the intended audience.
6. Monitoring Brand Reputation: Utilize ChatGPT to monitor brand reputation online, identifying and addressing potential reputation issues like negative reviews or social media mentions in a timely manner.
7. Evaluating Campaign Effectiveness: Engage ChatGPT to evaluate the effectiveness of marketing and advertising campaigns, generating questions or considerations related to metrics such as reach, engagement, conversion rates, or return on investment (ROI).

It's important to remember that while ChatGPT can be a valuable tool, it should not be the sole source of information or guidance. Cross-referencing insights and recommendations from ChatGPT with other sources such as industry reports or marketing experts ensures accuracy and relevance. By integrating ChatGPT's capabilities with other research methods, more effective marketing and advertising strategies can be developed to achieve business objectives and resonate with the target audience.

Content Creation for Marketing

Generating content for marketing purposes can be facilitated by using ChatGPT. Here's how you can leverage ChatGPT for this purpose:

1. Idea Generation: Utilize ChatGPT to brainstorm ideas for content that align with your marketing goals and target demographic. For instance, you can ask for blog post ideas for a beauty brand targeting millennials or video content suggestions for a new range of eco-friendly home products.
2. Crafting Brand Messaging: Seek assistance from ChatGPT in developing clear and compelling brand messages that connect with your audience.

Examples include defining key value propositions for a sustainable fashion brand or crafting effective taglines for a new line of organic baby products.

3. Social Media Content Creation: Employ ChatGPT to craft engaging and shareable social media content, including captions, hashtags, and image descriptions. For example, you can inquire about creative Instagram caption ideas for a new line of workout equipment or effective hashtags for a range of healthy snacks.
4. Writing Blog Posts or Articles: ChatGPT can aid in generating content ideas, structuring outlines, and providing informative insights for blog posts or articles. You might ask for tips on writing effective product review blog posts or the benefits of using natural ingredients in skincare products.
5. Email Newsletter Ideas: Use ChatGPT to generate content ideas for email newsletters that encourage audience engagement. This could involve coming up with engaging subject lines for a tech startup's weekly newsletter or effective calls-to-action for an e-commerce store's holiday sale newsletter.
6. Visual Content Design: ChatGPT can assist in designing visually appealing infographics or graphics that effectively convey your message. You might inquire about key statistics to include in an infographic about the benefits of meditation or creative designs for a Facebook ad promoting a new line of activewear.

It's essential to remember that while ChatGPT can be a valuable tool, it should not be the sole source of content creation ideas. It's important to validate insights and recommendations from ChatGPT with other sources such as customer feedback, competitor analysis, or advice from marketing experts. By combining ChatGPT's capabilities with other research methods, you can create marketing content that is both engaging and effective, resonating with your target audience and achieving your business objectives.

Engagement and Interaction with Customers

Enhancing customer engagement and interaction can be achieved through ChatGPT's capabilities, which include offering insights, recommendations, and tailored responses. Utilizing ChatGPT effectively involves several key strategies:

1. Tailoring interactions: Customize interactions with customers by leveraging ChatGPT to deliver pertinent information, suggestions, or responses based on their preferences, behaviors, or past interactions. For instance, inquire about personalized recommendations for a customer who recently bought a yoga mat or request customized responses for someone interested in eco-friendly products.
2. Providing useful information: Utilize ChatGPT to furnish customers with helpful information, such as product specifications, delivery details, or return policies, in response to their queries. Examples include asking about the dimensions of a new furniture line or the procedure for returning a defective item.
3. Offering support: Engage ChatGPT to provide support to customers by troubleshooting technical issues, addressing complaints, or offering guidance on product usage. For instance, seek steps to troubleshoot a mobile app issue or tips for resolving a delayed delivery complaint.
4. Generating tailored recommendations: Employ ChatGPT to generate personalized product recommendations based on customers' preferences, behaviors, or purchase history. Examples include requesting product suggestions for someone interested in organic skincare products or related items for a recent laptop purchaser.
5. Analyzing feedback: Leverage ChatGPT to analyze customer feedback, including reviews, ratings, and social media comments, to identify areas for improvement and enhance customer engagement.
6. Automating interactions: Utilize ChatGPT to automate customer interactions, such as through chatbots, email responses, or personalized

product recommendations, to enhance efficiency and scalability while maintaining customer satisfaction.

However, it's essential to remember that ChatGPT should complement human interaction and empathy in customer service. Balancing ChatGPT with human support ensures personalized and effective customer engagement. By integrating ChatGPT's capabilities with other customer service tools and strategies, businesses can foster long-term customer relationships and enhance overall satisfaction.

6

Customer Service Automation

Utilizing ChatGPT for customer service automation can offer numerous benefits, including increased efficiency, scalability, and consistency, as well as decreased costs and errors. Here's a breakdown of how you can leverage ChatGPT for automating customer service:

1. Develop chatbots: Chatbots powered by natural language processing and ChatGPT's capabilities can handle common customer inquiries, like product details, order status, or returns. These chatbots can be tailored for various platforms such as website chat, social media messaging, or mobile apps, enhancing accessibility and convenience.
2. Automate email responses: Utilize ChatGPT to automate email replies to customer queries, including order confirmations, shipping updates, or FAQs. This automation can lead to faster response times and reduced manual workload. ChatGPT can craft personalized responses based on customer information and past interactions, ensuring a tailored experience.
3. Offer self-service options: Leverage ChatGPT to create self-service features like knowledge base articles, FAQs, or tutorials, empowering customers to find solutions independently. This approach boosts efficiency and lightens the load on your customer service team.

4. Automate personalized recommendations: Use ChatGPT to generate tailored product suggestions for customers based on their preferences, behavior, and purchase history. This can enhance upselling and cross-selling opportunities, elevating the overall customer experience.
5. Analyze customer data: ChatGPT can aid in analyzing customer data such as purchase history, feedback, and behavior to uncover patterns, trends, and areas for improvement. This data-driven approach allows for optimization of the customer service automation strategy and prioritization of enhancement areas.

While ChatGPT can streamline customer service, it's crucial to strike a balance between automation and human support, ensuring a personalized and satisfactory experience. Chatbots and automated responses should offer value and convenience while maintaining quality and accuracy. Regular evaluation and optimization of the automation strategy based on customer feedback and data analysis are essential to ensure its effectiveness and relevance.

The Role of ChatGPT in Customer Support

ChatGPT can play a significant role in enhancing customer support by delivering efficient, tailored, and impactful assistance to customers. Here are ways you can utilize ChatGPT for customer support:

1. Automated FAQs: ChatGPT can aid in creating automated Frequently Asked Questions (FAQs) for customers, offering swift and accessible access to information. This can alleviate the workload of your customer support team while enabling customers to swiftly find the information they need.
2. Personalized recommendations: Utilize ChatGPT to produce personalized recommendations for customers based on their buying history, preferences, and behaviors. This can help customers discover new

products of interest and enrich their overall experience.

3. Natural language processing: Leveraging ChatGPT's natural language processing (NLP) abilities allows customers to engage with your support team in a conversational and intuitive manner. Customers can articulate their queries naturally, and ChatGPT can deliver accurate and relevant responses in real-time.

4. Social media monitoring: ChatGPT can aid in monitoring social media platforms for customer inquiries and grievances. By employing ChatGPT to scrutinize customer feedback, you can detect patterns, trends, and opportunities for enhancing customer support.

5. Automated responses: Employ ChatGPT to automate responses to customer inquiries, such as order confirmations, shipping notifications, or FAQs. This can enhance response times and alleviate the burden on your customer support team.

6. Chatbots: Chatbots can assist customers with routine inquiries, like product information, order status, or returns, utilizing natural language processing and ChatGPT's capabilities. You can develop chatbots for various channels, such as website chat, social media messaging, or mobile apps, to heighten accessibility and convenience for customers.

It's crucial to note that while ChatGPT can enhance customer support, it shouldn't substitute human interaction and empathy. Chatbots and automated responses should be designed to offer value and convenience to customers while upholding high standards of quality and accuracy. Additionally, it's essential to regularly assess and refine your ChatGPT-powered customer support strategy based on customer feedback and data analysis to ensure its efficacy and pertinence.

Setting Up Automated Customer Service

Below are the steps for establishing an automated customer service system using ChatGPT:

CHATGPT FOR ENTREPRENEURS: AUTOMATION AND OPTIMIZATION": EXPLORE HOW CHATGPT CAN BE USED TO IMPROVE EFFICIENCY IN THE ENTREPRENEURIAL CONTEXT.

1. Specify your objectives and goals for customer service: Determine what you aim to accomplish with automated customer service. Define key metrics like response time, customer satisfaction, and issue resolution rate, and pinpoint areas where automation can enhance customer support.

2. Select your customer service channels: Recognize the platforms your customers use to engage with your business, such as email, chat, social media, or phone, and decide which channels to automate.

3. Formulate your automation strategy: Create a plan for automating customer service that aligns with your business goals and customer requirements. Identify the types of inquiries suitable for automation, like FAQs, order tracking, or returns, and specify the responses that ChatGPT can generate.

4. Construct your ChatGPT models: Utilize a ChatGPT platform like GPT-3 to construct your models. Train these models on your existing customer support data, including common questions, support tickets, and customer feedback. Utilize ChatGPT to generate personalized responses based on customer data and past interactions for a tailored experience.

5. Execute your automation plan: Roll out your automated customer service across chosen channels, such as automated email responses, chatbots, or social media monitoring. Integrate ChatGPT with your customer service platform or connect it via an API to your website or mobile app.

6. Monitor and refine your automation strategy: Regularly oversee your automated customer service to ensure it delivers value and meets your goals. Use ChatGPT to analyze customer feedback and data, identifying areas for enhancement and refining your automation strategy accordingly.

It's important to note that while ChatGPT can aid in automating customer service, it shouldn't entirely replace human interaction and empathy. Chatbots and automated responses should prioritize providing value and convenience to customers while maintaining quality and accuracy. Regular evaluation and optimization of your ChatGPT-driven customer service strategy based on customer feedback and data analysis are crucial to ensuring its efficacy and relevance over time.

7

ChatGPT for Product Development

Utilizing ChatGPT for product development can be highly beneficial, offering insights, recommendations, and evaluations across various stages of the process. Here are several ways to employ ChatGPT in this context:

1. Generating Ideas: Tap into ChatGPT to brainstorm fresh product concepts drawing from customer input, industry trends, or market analysis. For instance, seek input on innovative ideas for eco-friendly home goods or distinctive features for a fitness brand's mobile app.

2. Design Evaluation: Seek ChatGPT's input on refining product designs, encompassing aspects like packaging, user interface, or functionalities, to enhance user experience and aesthetic appeal. Examples include seeking improvements for sustainable clothing lines or design suggestions for smart home gadgets.

3. User Testing Support: Utilize ChatGPT to assist in crafting and executing user testing strategies to gauge product usability, functionality, and satisfaction levels. This could involve drafting survey questions for a mobile app or identifying crucial metrics for assessing beauty product performance.

4. Product Naming: Task ChatGPT with generating catchy, memorable product names tailored to your target audience. Whether it's natural skincare items or organic pet food, seek out effective naming suggestions.

5. Crafting Marketing Messages: Collaborate with ChatGPT to craft persuasive marketing messages that effectively communicate your product's value proposition to your audience. Whether it's sustainable cleaning products or energy drinks, seek guidance on key value propositions and impactful taglines.

It's important to remember that while ChatGPT offers valuable assistance, it shouldn't replace human expertise and creativity in product development. Balancing its use with other research methods, such as customer feedback and competitor analysis, ensures accuracy, relevance, and creativity in product development endeavors. By harnessing ChatGPT's capabilities alongside human insights and diverse research methods, you can create innovative, impactful products that meet customer needs and drive business growth.

Brainstorming Product Features with ChatGPT

Utilizing ChatGPT for brainstorming product features offers a valuable approach, drawing upon a spectrum of creative, varied, and pertinent ideas rooted in customer input, market trends, and industry knowledge. Consider these strategies for leveraging ChatGPT in this process:

1. Establish product objectives: Begin by defining the goals and objectives of your product, focusing on delivering value to your customers. Understand your target audience, their needs, and pain points to guide your brainstorming endeavors.
2. Pose open-ended queries: Prompt ChatGPT with open-ended questions to elicit a wide array of responses, avoiding constraints on creativity. For

instance, inquire about potential features for a beauty brand's mobile app or innovative functionalities for a new line of smart home devices.
3. Integrate diverse perspectives: Engage ChatGPT to generate ideas from various viewpoints, including customer feedback, competitor analysis, and industry insights. Blend these perspectives to spark fresh and inventive concepts for product features.
4. Emphasize user experience: Task ChatGPT with suggesting enhancements that enhance user experience, such as streamlining usage, enriching functionality, or personalizing features. Focus on addressing customer pain points and delivering value.
5. Prioritize concepts: Utilize ChatGPT to rank ideas based on feasibility, impact, and relevance. Concentrate on those with the most potential impact, considering resource and time constraints for implementation.

It's essential to remember that while ChatGPT is a valuable tool, it shouldn't supplant human creativity and expertise in product feature ideation. Maintaining a balance between ChatGPT and other research methodologies like customer feedback, competitor analysis, and expert insights ensures the accuracy, relevance, and innovation of your product development endeavors. By harnessing the capabilities of ChatGPT alongside traditional research methods and human knowledge, you can cultivate innovative and impactful product features that resonate with your customers and drive business growth.

User Experience Design and ChatGPT

Leveraging ChatGPT in user experience (UX) design offers valuable insights across various UX domains like user research, interface design, usability testing, and user engagement. Here's how you can utilize ChatGPT effectively:

1. User Research: Utilize ChatGPT to formulate survey and interview questions, as well as create user personas. For instance, seek guidance on crafting questions for a mobile app survey or defining characteristics for eco-friendly product personas.
2. User Interface Design: Solicit ChatGPT's input on aspects like color palettes, typography, layout, and navigation to enhance usability and visual appeal. For example, request design suggestions for a fitness app or improvements for smart home device interfaces.
3. Usability Testing: Engage ChatGPT to design surveys for gathering feedback on product usability and satisfaction, and inquire about metrics for assessing usability in testing sessions.
4. User Engagement: Generate ideas from ChatGPT to boost user engagement through gamification, personalization, or social sharing strategies. For instance, explore ways to enhance engagement for sustainable clothing lines or incentivize interaction in mobile apps.
5. Accessibility: Seek ChatGPT's feedback on accessibility features like closed captions and screen readers to enhance product usability for users with disabilities.

It's crucial to remember that while ChatGPT can offer valuable insights, it should complement, not replace, human expertise and creativity in UX design. Balancing ChatGPT with traditional research methods like user testing and expert evaluation ensures the accuracy, relevance, and creativity of UX efforts. By integrating ChatGPT's capabilities with human expertise and diverse research methods, you can develop user-centric products that resonate with your audience and drive business growth.

8

Improving Operational Efficiency

Utilizing ChatGPT can significantly enhance operational efficiency through its ability to offer insights, recommendations, and evaluations across various operational domains, including workflow enhancement, process automation, resource management, and performance evaluation. Here are some strategies for leveraging ChatGPT to boost operational efficiency:

1. Streamlining Workflow: Employ ChatGPT to scrutinize your workflow, pinpointing areas of inefficiency and congestion. Solicit ChatGPT's input on streamlining workflow by suggesting task reorganization, refining communication channels, or automating repetitive tasks.
2. Automating Processes: Task ChatGPT with identifying processes amenable to automation, aiming to minimize manual labor and errors. For instance, inquire about automating tasks within the customer service department or tools for automating inventory management.
3. Optimizing Resource Allocation: Utilize ChatGPT to assess resource allocation, identifying wastage and inefficiencies. Seek recommendations from ChatGPT on reallocating resources to priority tasks, outsourcing non-core functions, or trimming unnecessary expenditures.
4. Enhancing Performance Measurement: Seek insights from ChatGPT on performance metrics to gauge and enhance operational efficiency.

Examples include key metrics for monitoring manufacturing processes or performance measurement tools for project management.
5. Informed Decision-Making: Engage ChatGPT to aid in informed decision-making through data analysis and industry insights. Seek guidance on decision-making frameworks such as SWOT analysis, cost-benefit analysis, or risk analysis.

It's essential to remember that while ChatGPT is a valuable tool, it should not supplant human expertise and judgment. Balancing ChatGPT with other research methods like data analysis, expert consultation, or stakeholder input ensures accuracy, relevance, and creativity in operational efficiency endeavors. By integrating ChatGPT's capabilities with human expertise and diverse research methods, operational efficiency and productivity can be enhanced while minimizing costs and risks.

Utilizing ChatGPT for Process Automation

Employing ChatGPT in process automation can offer valuable assistance through insights, recommendations, and evaluations across various automation stages like process identification, design, optimization, and monitoring. Here's how you can utilize ChatGPT for automating processes:

1. Process Identification: Utilize ChatGPT to pinpoint tasks suitable for automation, such as repetitive duties, data input, or reporting. For instance, inquire about potential automatable processes within departments like customer service or marketing.
2. Process Design: Seek ChatGPT's guidance in crafting automated processes that prioritize efficiency, accuracy, and scalability. For example, ask about automation tools for inventory management or optimal workflows for production processes.
3. Process Optimization: Leverage ChatGPT to scrutinize automated

processes, pinpointing areas of inefficiency, errors, or delays. Solicit suggestions from ChatGPT to streamline processes, like reducing manual intervention or enhancing data quality.
4. Process Monitoring: Task ChatGPT with overseeing and evaluating the performance of automated processes. Use it to track key metrics such as cycle time or error rates, and set up alerts for subpar performance.
5. Integration: Employ ChatGPT to seamlessly integrate automated processes with existing systems and tools like CRM or ERP. Request insights on integration strategies and compatible tools to enhance workflow efficiency.

It's essential to remember that while ChatGPT is a valuable tool, it shouldn't replace human expertise in process automation. Balancing its use with other research methods and human judgment ensures the accuracy and relevance of automation efforts. By harnessing ChatGPT alongside traditional methods and human insight, you can streamline processes, minimize errors, and enhance efficiency and scalability.

Enhancing Workflow Efficiency

Leveraging ChatGPT can significantly enhance workflow efficiency by offering insights, recommendations, and evaluations across various workflow components, including task management, communication, teamwork, and resource utilization. Below are ways to employ ChatGPT for streamlining workflows:

1. Task Organization: Utilize ChatGPT to assess tasks and pinpoint areas of inefficiency, redundancy, or backlog. Solicit ChatGPT's input on organizing tasks, such as prioritization, creating templates, or segmenting tasks based on urgency and significance.
2. Communication: Seek ChatGPT's assistance in refining team commu-

nication by receiving guidance on effective communication practices like employing collaboration tools, scheduling regular meetings, or establishing communication protocols.
3. Collaboration: Harness ChatGPT's capabilities to enhance teamwork by acquiring recommendations for improved collaboration practices, such as delineating roles and responsibilities, leveraging collaboration tools, or fostering a collaborative environment.
4. Resource Allocation: Engage ChatGPT to optimize resource allocation by obtaining suggestions for better resource management practices, such as reallocating resources to high-priority tasks, outsourcing non-core tasks, or trimming unnecessary expenses.
5. Performance Evaluation: Utilize ChatGPT for evaluating and refining workflow performance by seeking suggestions on key performance indicators (KPIs) to monitor, such as cycle time, lead time, or task completion rate.

It's essential to remember that while ChatGPT offers valuable insights, it shouldn't replace human expertise and judgment in workflow optimization. A balanced approach involving stakeholder consultation, expert review, or process analysis alongside ChatGPT ensures the accuracy, relevance, and innovation of workflow optimization endeavors. By synergizing ChatGPT's capabilities with other research methods and human expertise, you can enhance productivity, efficiency, and quality in workflows while mitigating errors, delays, and costs.

9

ChatGPT for HR and Team Management

Utilizing ChatGPT can be advantageous for HR and team management as it offers insights, advice, and assessments on various facets of HR and team management, including recruitment, employee engagement, performance management, and team cohesion. Below are ways to leverage ChatGPT for HR and team management:

1. Recruitment: Employ ChatGPT to aid in recruitment tasks by suggesting improvements for job descriptions, candidate screening methods, and interview inquiries. For instance, seek guidance on effective interview questions for hiring a project manager or crafting job descriptions for software engineers.
2. Employee engagement: Solicit ChatGPT's recommendations for enhancing employee engagement through initiatives like recognition programs, team-building exercises, or wellness activities. Examples include strategies for improving engagement among remote teams or suggesting enjoyable team-building activities for small startups.
3. Performance management: Utilize ChatGPT to support performance management endeavors by seeking advice on evaluation techniques, feedback delivery, and goal establishment. For example, inquire about best practices for conducting performance evaluations for sales teams or effective feedback methods for remote teams.

4. Team building: Request ChatGPT's suggestions for team-building activities that foster collaboration, communication, and creativity. Examples include activities to enhance collaboration across different departments or creative ideas for newly formed teams.
5. Professional development: Harness ChatGPT's capabilities to aid in professional development by seeking guidance on training programs, mentorship opportunities, and career planning. Examples include effective training programs for software developers or best practices for mentorship programs in startup environments.

It is essential to remember that ChatGPT should complement rather than replace human expertise and judgment in HR and team management. Balancing the use of ChatGPT with other research methods, such as stakeholder consultations, expert reviews, or data analysis, ensures the accuracy, relevance, and creativity of HR and team management efforts. By integrating ChatGPT's capabilities with other research methods and human expertise, organizations can enhance HR and team management practices to improve employee satisfaction, productivity, and retention.

Automated Staff Onboarding

Utilizing ChatGPT for automated staff onboarding can be highly beneficial, as it can offer insights, recommendations, and evaluations on various facets of the onboarding procedure, spanning paperwork, training, orientation, and team assimilation. Here are some strategies for employing ChatGPT in automated staff onboarding:

1. Paperwork: Utilize ChatGPT to streamline paperwork processes by receiving guidance on digital forms, e-signature platforms, and document management systems. For instance, inquire about effective e-signature tools for onboarding paperwork or seek advice on crafting

digital onboarding forms.

2. Training: Seek ChatGPT's assistance in recommending automated training resources, such as video tutorials, online courses, or interactive quizzes. For instance, request suggestions on pertinent video tutorials for a software developer onboarding program or seek guidance on developing online courses for a sales team.
3. Orientation: Employ ChatGPT to automate orientation sessions by obtaining recommendations for virtual onboarding sessions, video introductions, or gamified activities. For example, ask about effective virtual onboarding sessions for remote teams or inquire about creative methods for introducing new hires to company culture.
4. Team Integration: Consult ChatGPT for suggestions on automated team integration practices, including virtual meet-and-greets, buddy systems, or collaborative projects. For example, seek advice on implementing effective buddy programs in a startup setting or inquire about best practices for organizing virtual team-building exercises.

It's crucial to remember that while ChatGPT can enhance the efficiency of employee onboarding, it shouldn't replace human interaction entirely. Balancing ChatGPT with human-led efforts like mentorship, coaching, and socialization ensures a well-rounded and personalized onboarding experience. By combining ChatGPT's capabilities with human-led initiatives, organizations can automate onboarding processes to reduce manual labor, errors, and expenses, while simultaneously enhancing efficiency, precision, and scalability.

Team Communication and Coordination

Utilizing ChatGPT for team communication and coordination can be highly beneficial, offering insights, advice, and evaluations across various facets including tools, communication practices, conflict resolution, and goal alignment. Here are some practical ways to employ ChatGPT for enhancing team communication and coordination:

1. Tools and platforms: Engage ChatGPT to recommend communication and collaboration tools or platforms aimed at boosting team efficiency. This could include suggestions for project management software, team messaging applications, or video conferencing solutions. For instance, inquire about effective team messaging apps for remote teams or seek guidance on optimizing project management software for cross-functional teams.
2. Communication practices: Utilize ChatGPT to refine communication practices within your team by receiving suggestions on fostering better habits such as clear messaging, active listening, and providing timely feedback. Seek advice on effective communication habits tailored to your team's context, like those pertinent to sales teams or remote meeting best practices.
3. Conflict resolution: Solicit ChatGPT's input on strategies and techniques for resolving conflicts within the team, encompassing approaches like active listening, compromise, or mediation. Seek recommendations on conflict resolution techniques suited for specific team dynamics, such as cross-functional teams or startup environments.
4. Goal alignment: Leverage ChatGPT to aid in aligning team goals and objectives by obtaining suggestions for improved goal-setting practices, such as SMART goals, OKRs, or KPIs. Ask for advice on effective goal-setting practices tailored to your team's domain, like marketing teams, or insights on measuring team performance, particularly within software development teams.

It's essential to remember that while ChatGPT can offer valuable support, it should not replace human interaction and feedback entirely. Balancing the use of ChatGPT with human-led efforts such as team-building activities, coaching, and mentorship is crucial for ensuring effective team communication and coordination. By harnessing ChatGPT's capabilities in conjunction with human-led initiatives, you can enhance team productivity, creativity, and overall satisfaction.

10

Looking Ahead: ChatGPT and the Future of Entrepreneurship

As artificial intelligence progresses and becomes more accessible, ChatGPT stands to become an increasingly valuable asset for entrepreneurs. With its capacity to generate innovative ideas, analyze data, and offer insights, ChatGPT can aid entrepreneurs in identifying fresh business prospects, refining operations, and enhancing customer interaction. Here are some potential applications for ChatGPT in the entrepreneurial realm:

1. Tailored customer experiences: ChatGPT can assist entrepreneurs in customizing their interactions with customers by delivering personalized recommendations, responses, and solutions based on customer data and preferences.
2. Precision marketing: Entrepreneurs can utilize ChatGPT to craft highly targeted marketing campaigns by examining customer behavior, interests, and demographics, thereby gaining insights into the most effective messaging and channels to reach their desired audience.
3. Predictive analysis: ChatGPT can enable entrepreneurs to predict trends, forecast demand, and pinpoint potential risks and opportunities by analyzing data from various sources and providing insights into future

market and customer behavior.

4. Automated workflows: ChatGPT can aid entrepreneurs in automating repetitive, time-consuming, and error-prone business tasks such as data entry, invoicing, and inventory management by suggesting tools and strategies to streamline and optimize operations.
5. Collaborative innovation: Entrepreneurs can leverage ChatGPT to foster collaborative innovation by providing a platform for employees, customers, and partners to exchange ideas, feedback, and insights, leading to the generation of new solutions and products.

However, like any technology, there are potential risks and challenges associated with the use of ChatGPT in entrepreneurship, such as privacy concerns, bias and ethical issues, and the risk of overreliance on AI-generated insights. It is crucial for entrepreneurs to strike a balance between leveraging ChatGPT's capabilities and human expertise, staying informed about the latest developments and best practices in AI and entrepreneurship. By integrating ChatGPT's capabilities with other research methods and human expertise, entrepreneurs can establish innovative, sustainable, and socially responsible businesses that fulfill the needs and expectations of their customers and stakeholders.

Current Trends and Future Predictions

Present trends in entrepreneurship and AI indicate a continuous surge in the utilization of ChatGPT and similar AI resources in the forthcoming years. Here are some ongoing trends and forthcoming projections pertaining to ChatGPT and entrepreneurship:

1. Surge in AI-driven customer service: The proliferation of chatbots and virtual assistants is prompting more businesses to embrace AI-driven customer service for enhancing customer engagement and satisfaction.

ChatGPT and other AI tools can augment these systems, making them more personalized and responsive to customer needs.
2. Escalating demand for AI-generated content: As businesses prioritize content marketing, the need for AI-generated content like blog posts, social media updates, and product descriptions is anticipated to rise. ChatGPT and other AI tools can automate and optimize content creation, enhancing efficiency and effectiveness.
3. Increased AI integration in recruitment and HR: Faced with stiff competition for talent, companies are turning to AI-powered recruitment and HR tools to streamline hiring processes and enhance employee engagement and retention. ChatGPT and other AI tools can aid in identifying top candidates, offering personalized training, and facilitating team communication and collaboration.
4. Emphasis on ethical and responsible AI: With AI's expanding influence in entrepreneurship and society, there's a growing awareness of associated risks and challenges. Ethical and responsible AI practices such as transparency, fairness, and privacy protection are likely to receive increased attention.
5. Advancements in natural language processing and chatbot technology: Progress in natural language processing and chatbot technology is expected to enhance the sophistication of ChatGPT and similar AI tools, enabling better understanding and response to human language and behavior. This could lead to novel applications in fields like mental health, education, and personal finance.

In essence, the future of ChatGPT and entrepreneurship will likely witness heightened integration and collaboration between AI and human expertise, as entrepreneurs strive to harness AI technology innovatively to enhance their businesses.

Ethical Considerations and Responsible Use of AI in Business

In the realm of business, as AI technology becomes increasingly prevalent, it's imperative for business owners to contemplate the ethical ramifications of its utilization and embrace practices that uphold responsibility, ensuring AI is wielded in a manner that's equitable, transparent, and socially conscientious. Below are outlined several ethical considerations and responsible practices for entrepreneurs employing AI in their business endeavors:

1. Mitigating bias and discrimination: A pivotal ethical concern when employing AI in business operations is the risk of bias and discrimination. To sidestep these issues, entrepreneurs must ensure that their AI systems are crafted and trained using diverse, representative datasets, and regularly assess their performance to identify and rectify any emerging biases.
2. Fostering transparency and accountability: Business owners utilizing AI must be forthcoming about the design of their systems, the data employed, and the decision-making process. Moreover, they should establish clear avenues for feedback and recourse, empowering customers and stakeholders to contest decisions made by AI systems when necessary.
3. Safeguarding privacy and data security: Entrepreneurs leveraging AI must implement robust measures to safeguard the privacy and security of their customers' data, including stringent encryption protocols, access controls, and data retention policies. Compliance with pertinent data protection laws and regulations is essential, alongside transparent communication regarding data collection, usage, and sharing practices.
4. Addressing the implications for employment: The integration of AI into business operations has the potential to automate numerous tasks and roles currently undertaken by humans. Entrepreneurs should be cognizant of the potential impact on employment and take proactive

measures to retrain and reskill employees whose positions may be jeopardized by AI adoption.
5. Championing ethical AI research and development: Entrepreneurs leveraging AI should actively support and advance ethical research and development initiatives, particularly those focused on bias mitigation, explainability, and fairness. Engagement with relevant stakeholders, including customers, employees, and regulators, is crucial to ensuring that AI systems are developed and utilized in a socially responsible manner that aligns with public values.

By embracing these ethical considerations and responsible practices, entrepreneurs can ensure that their utilization of AI in business is ethical, just, and in harmony with societal values, while simultaneously harnessing the full potential benefits of AI technology for their enterprises and stakeholders.

The ideal prompt for the advertiser:

Compose a prompt in GPT Chat resembling the following exactly as it appears below. Experiment with altering the terms enclosed in quotation marks to tailor the content to your preferences. Keep in mind, if you're in the advertising field, this prompt is tailored specifically for you and can be a potent tool if utilized effectively!

Sales Page Prompt:
   Assume the role of an advertiser and craft an informational-themed sales page titled "The Ultimate Bike You'll Ever Own," targeting an audience of "males above 50," with the objective of persuading the reader to make a purchase. The structure of the article should include: a title, introduction, 1 H2 section, and 1 H3 section. The H3 sections will function as subsections of the H2 sections. Format the narrative using markdown. Employ a professional writing style, an engaging tone, and an informal communicative approach.

Market Research Prompt:
   Act as an analyst, and I'll assume the role of an advertiser. My aim is to promote a "bicycle" product, so conduct thorough market research to furnish me with all the essential details that will facilitate the creation of my advertisement. This informative article should be comprehensive, detailed, and structured with a title, introduction, 1 H2 section, and 1 H3 section. The H3 sections will serve as subsections of the H2 sections. Format the article using markdown. Employ an analytical writing style, evoke a formal

ambiance, and adopt a professional communicative tone.

Newsletter Prompt:

Imagine yourself as a social media manager, and I'll assume the role of a business owner with a focus on "yoga." Develop a detailed newsletter publication plan designed to retain customers. The plan should be expansive, covering various aspects. Its structure should include: a title, introduction, 1 H2 section, and 1 H3 section. The H3 sections will function as subsections of the H2 sections. Format the content using markdown. Utilize an analytical writing style, maintain a formal tone, and employ a professional communicative register.

www.ingramcontent.com/pod-product-compliance
Lightning Source LLC
LaVergne TN
LVHW020441080526
838202LV00055B/5297